IMAGES
of America

CANISTEO

In 1934, civil engineer Harry Smith, along with his brother-in-law Edwin M. Childs, conceived and planned the living sign. Noted in Robert Ripley's *Believe It or Not* as the world's largest living sign, the sign is planted in Scotch pine trees and is 60 feet by 400 feet. In 2004, it was added to both the New York State and National Register of Historic Places. (Courtesy of the Kanestio Historical Society.)

ON THE COVER: This photograph was taken sometime after 1892; according to the sign in front of the hardware store, the gathering was some type of contest. Most of the teams in the foreground haul McCormick farm equipment, while the ones in the background are mostly buckboards. The judges are on either side of the front two teams. (Courtesy of the Kanestio Historical Society.)

IMAGES
of *America*

CANISTEO

Steve Cotton

ARCADIA
PUBLISHING

Published by Arcadia Publishing
Charleston, South Carolina

Library of Congress Control Number: 2012953750

For all general information, please contact Arcadia Publishing:
Telephone 843-853-2070
Fax 843-853-0044
E-mail sales@arcadiapublishing.com
For customer service and orders:
Toll-Free 1-888-313-2665

Visit us on the Internet at www.arcadiapublishing.com

*To Colby and Amelia: embrace the future, but do not forget the past.
Thanks for your support.*

CONTENTS

Foreword   6

Acknowledgments   7

Introduction   8

1.   The Village   9

2.   The 1887 and 1898 Canisteo Arches Firemen's Parades   61

3.   Gas Stations and Garages   77

4.   Schools   85

5.   Cemeteries   95

6.   Churches   99

7.   The Town   105

8.   About the Kanestio Historical Society   127

FOREWORD

It is well documented that the first inhabitants of the Canisteo Valley were an unscrupulous bunch: renegade Indians of different tribes, outlaws of various nationalities, and other undesirables. The settlement, first known as Kanestio Castle, flourished as a refuge for these undesirables for nearly a century. In 1764, after the murder of two traders from Hudson at Kanestio Castle, a large expedition led by Capt. Andrew Montour set off to avenge the murders. As a result, Kanestio Castle was burned completely, and its inhabitants scattered.

For nearly a quarter century thereafter, the Canisteo Valley lay virtually uninhabited. In the fall of 1789, the first permanent settlers arrived in the valley to make their homes and farm the land. These individuals—Uriah Stevens Sr., Benjamin Crosby, and their families—came from Newtown, near Elmira, to take possession of the colony.

In the following decades, the Town of Canisteo prospered and grew. More and more settlers, after hearing of the beautiful and fertile valley, came and established farms and, businesses to market the goods produced. The Erie Railroad came to Canisteo in 1851, which opened the valley to more markets. In the last half of the 19th century and well into the 20th century, Canisteo was home to several factories, manufacturing items from shoes to tables to iron goods.

Today, industry in Canisteo is virtually nonexistent, but many farms, raising both cattle and crops, are still operating. Most working residents travel to other communities for employment, while children enjoy the opportunities provided by the excellent schools. Retirees enjoy many activities in the quiet solitude and eternal beauty that abounds in the town and the valley.

Regardless of what the future holds for Canisteo and the surrounding communities, we can be sure that this valley will always be appreciated for its beauty and natural resources. Having been born, raised, and currently living in Canisteo, it is my hope that our proud community continues to thrive as it has and be a place that we can all call home.

—William K. Tucker
Mayor, Village of Canisteo

ACKNOWLEDGMENTS

As a child, many of us neighborhood kids would sit on Pete Howland's front porch, where we learned terms like "thank-you-mom," a common local phrase meaning there was a drain ditch across the road, and listened to stories of bygone days. My teenage years found me cleaning house for Ada (Stephens) Hallett on the Narrows farm. Many of the neighborhood boys worked for her husband, Walt, in the hay fields; when Walt needed an extra hand on the farm, I would join the other boys in the hayloft. The times spent with Pete Howland and Ada Hallett inspired my interest in our local history, and I owe a lot to these two neighbors.

In 1990, I joined the Kanestio Historical Society, where I was taken under the wings of Virginia Dickey and Kay Bancroft. I have held many positions at the society over the years, sat in many meetings, and learned a lot about both the society and the rich history of the Canisteo community from these two ladies. These are the people that planted the seeds that made this book possible.

Many of the photographs herein are courtesy of the Kanestio Historical Society (KHS). I would like to also acknowledge our county historian, Twila O'Dell (TO), for her help making this project a success and sharing photographs. Thanks to John Babbitt for opening up the archives at the Canisteo Fire Department (CFD) and our town historian, George Dickey (GD), for sharing not only photographs, but also knowledge of local history.

Photographs were also provided by Cindy Creeley (CC), Dave Harding (DH), Joan Coombs (JC), and Richard Stewart (RS). The remaining photographs are from my personal files (SC). Remy Thurston, my editor at Arcadia Publishing, was also a great help in making this book possible.

Lastly, I want to thank my wife, Connie, for her patience and support in my love of our rich local history.

INTRODUCTION

As one walks around Cy's Shurfine on Main Street, many enlargements of old photographs depict the history of Canisteo. The photographs selected for this book were chosen to tell the story of our community in images not widely seen.

In the late 1700s and early 1800s, the first families in the area depended on farming and lumbering. The Canisteo River provided a way to ship products to the markets in the Susquehanna River water basin.

The village of Canisteo was known first as Bennettsville and consisted of a few houses and the rather large Canisteo House hotel. After the Erie Railroad was built due to the lack of space between the tracks and the river at Canisteo Center (now Carson), the depot was placed up the river. Railroad Avenue (now Depot Street) was built to connect the depot with the hotel, and a large community sprang up as a result, with many businesses and stores opening, as well as more hotels. A photography shop and newspaper office opened around 1870, relaying the happenings of both the town and the world to locals. A second railroad, the New York & Pennsylvania, connected with the Erie at Canisteo, opening up markets as far away as Pennsylvania. In the 1890s, trolley service began between Canisteo and Hornell.

In 1887 and 1898, Canisteo hosted two firemen's conventions, and local photographer A.B. Stebbins took many rare photographs of the Canisteo Arches, which were created by firemen and local businesses to decorate the town for the occasion. Floods were also photographed.

The 1900s brought the age of the automobile, prompting 14 places to install gas pumps, along with a few dealerships and mechanical garages. Education was important to the residents, with the main school district in the village and several rural schoolhouses providing places for education, as well as community meeting places. Places of worship and burial grounds still dot the rural areas. This book provides a visual look into our past.

One

THE VILLAGE

Albert Benton "A.B." Stebbins, the son of photographer Benton Pixley Stebbins and his photographer wife, Sarah Ann, moved to Canisteo in 1879 when he was 29. He had learned photography from his parents, and, throughout his career, he captured the life of what became his hometown: Canisteo. Most of the photographs in this book were taken by him. (KHS.)

This 1951 view looks east over the village and down the Canisteo River Valley. Teddy and Kathy Sick are seen here with their dog Pal on the hill where Square Woods Drive is today. The Erie tacks are seen in the distance, making their way through the foothills of the Appalachian Mountains,

while, on the right, Bennett's Creek wraps its way around the base of one of the hills. The town is 1,135 feet above sea level. (KHS.)

Much is owed to this man, William M. Stuart, who worked as a schoolteacher, postmaster, and state senator. More importantly, he recorded Canisteo's history in the book *Stories of the Kanestio Valley*. The stories first appeared in the *Canisteo Times* and then in book form. The third edition can still be purchased today and is used as the textbook in the high school's local history class. (KHS.)

A Pleased Customer Pleases Us.

We Want You To Call And Will Try To Make Your Visit Pleasant.

You'll Like What We Sell You, And Be Benefitted By It.

TIME TABLES.

ERIE R. R.

Passenger Trains Leave Canisteo as follows:

GOING WEST.

a. m.	p. m.
No. 7—8:00	No. 17— 4:42
" 25—11:20	" 19—10:46

GOING EAST.

a. m.	p. m.
No. 20— 5:43	No. 14—2:24
" 18— 8:08	" 24—4:18
" 2—10:44	" 8—8:24

N. Y. & P. R. R.

Passenger Trains Leave Canisteo as follows:

GOING SOUTH.

a m.	p. m.
No. 2—9:15	No. 4—5:45
No. 6—6:30 a. m	

ARRIVING FROM SOUTH.

a. m.	p. m.
No. 1—8:55	No. 3—3:40
No. 5—3:15 p. m.	

H. & C. E. R. R.

Cars Leave Canisteo as follows:

MORNING,

6:20,   7:30,   9:05,   10:15,
11:00,   11:35.

AFTERNOON.

12:45, 1:30, 2:15, 3:00, 3:45, 4:25,
5:03, 6:10, 7:00, 7:45, 8:30,
9:00, 9:50, 11:00.

It's The Price That Appeals To You.

This Brasted's meat market business card from around 1900 had the timetables for the Erie Railroad, the New York & Pennsylvania Railroad (NY&P), and the Hornellsville & Canisteo electric trolley. The depot was busy each day; the Erie had 10 passenger trains arriving and departing each day, the NY&P had 3, and the trolley had 20. (RS.)

The Erie Bridge is seen here spanning the Canisteo River. This photograph, taken from what is known as Indian Ledge, offers a bird's-eye view of Canisteo and the valley. The Presbyterian and Methodist church steeples are in the background, and the Page Hotel, a barn, and a farmhouse are perched on the riverbank. (SC.)

The old depot and Agway facility is on the left, with the Wells Brothers sign factory on the right. The Wells factory originality opened for business in 1955, leasing a building on Fifth Street. The company purchased this building, the former home of Newark Milk & Cream Company, in 1967. (KHS.)

This is the only photograph of the original Erie Railroad depot after it burned in the late 1800s. The station agent had living quarters on the second floor. The main tracks ran on the backside; the tracks in the foreground are the yard tracks. A worker is on the communication pole directly behind the depot. (KHS.)

After the original depot burned, it was replaced by the one seen here. A steam-powered passenger train approaches from the west, just a few men wait for its arrival, and the baggage cart sits empty. The signal tower is on the right. Depot Street, originally called Railroad Avenue, was constructed as a direct route from the Canisteo House hotel to the depot. (SC.)

Levi S. Davis bought this boot and shoe factory from Isaac Allison in 1870. The factory, which specialized in children's shoes, was on the lower end of Depot Street, near what is now the village highway shop. Notice the workers hanging out of the second-floor windows. The short-lived American Silk Lace Company was across the street. (KHS.)

The workers and management of the Steuben Lumber & Furniture Co. posed for this photograph around 1880. Everyone had to stay perfectly still for the camera; however, no one told the horse, and he moved his head, blurring the picture. The second and third floors of the old factory, as well as the smokestack, have long been gone. (KHS.)

Joe Brasted, known as "Joe the Drayman," poses for a photograph with a load of masonry blocks in front of the Steuben Lumber and Furniture Co. on Depot Street. Next to him are a boxcar and a pile of lumber. The Erie Railroad tracks crossed the river and met with the New York & Pennsylvania rails, making it easy for the businesses on Depot Street to get their wares to market. (KHS.)

The Voorhis planing mill, seen here from the back, was at the present site of the Depot Street trailer park. Large piles of lumber can be seen to the left. The Canisteo Sash & Door Company took over the facility in 1885. The larger square building to the right is the Henry Carter & Son foundry. (KHS.)

Prices given on Application.

No. 17.   No. 18.

These two photographs show sample inventory found in the 1885 catalog of the Canisteo Sash & Door Company. After taking over the former Voorhis planing mill on Depot Street, the company enlarged the building and updated the machinery. Besides doors of various sizes and styles, it also manufactured sashes, shutters, blinds, elbow and back linings, soffits, cupboard and closet doors, balusters, newel posts, and stair rails. The company advertised that they carried a complete line of pine lumber at all times and shipped to New York, Philadelphia, and southern and foreign markets. (Both, SC.)

For Sizes, Prices, etc., see Page 15.

Front Doors, in Pairs.

$1\frac{1}{2}$ and $1\frac{7}{8}$ inches thick.

These workers at the Henry Carter & Son foundry stopped work to pose for the photographer. The foundry, founded in 1873, manufactured steam engines, reversible plows, cultivators, potato diggers, land rollers, kettles, sleigh and wagon shoes, post mauls, hay rakes, root cutters, stump machines, pulleys, hangers, and shafting. In 1890, the foundry employed 10 men. (KHS.)

These employees of the Henry Carter & Son foundry appear to be working on a boiler for a steam engine. North Street was once named Carter Street, as most of the homes were built as tenant houses for the employees of the foundry. The Henry Carter residence was at the corner of Greenwood and East Academy Streets. (KHS.)

Railroads were a big business because they were how many small towns received and shipped supplies. The loading and unloading was manual labor, providing jobs for local residents. These men unload coal from a New York Central & Hudson railcar at the New York & Pennsylvania depot in Canisteo. (KHS.)

Dr. S.G. Williamson purchased a total of five shares of stock in the newly formed Thomas Spring and Gear Co. in October 1906. This certifies three of the shares. Charles L. Thomas of Canisteo patented his invention of springs for cycle cars. The company opened for business in March 1908 in the former Tucker button factory on Depot Street, making shock absorbers for Ford cars. (SC.)

This group of 11 women and 13 men poses outside the basket factory on Depot Street. The factory made many types of baskets, including berry and picnic baskets. The Up-To-Date Advertising Co. took over the facility in 1906. (KHS.)

Half of this railroad crossing sign is broken off. The New York & Pennsylvania tracks crossed Depot Street and wrapped around the piles of wood leading to the Up-To-Date factory. On February 11 and 12 in 1921, the factory burned in a fire that took two days to extinguish. (SC.)

The front office of the Up-To-Date Advertising Co. had gaslights hanging from the wall on the left and early electric lights suspended from the ceiling. The safe seen here has two company names on it: York Safe and Lock Co. and Hatch & Taylor Safe Co. The three female employees are all sitting at typewriters. (KHS.)

J.C. Kenyon and J.T. Ramsey ordered a large quantity of "For Sale" signs from the Up-To-Date Advertising Co., as seen in this rare photograph of the printing room with a stencil hanging from the ceiling. The foremen have button-down shirts with ties, while the workers wear aprons at their workstations. (KHS.)

This farmhouse and barn, situated on the riverbank next to the railroad depot, are surrounded by standing water after a flood. The Erie tracks crossed the river between the small building and the barn, allowing Depot Street businesses shipping access. (KHS.)

The Depot Street river bridge can be seen at the far end of the street as the floodwaters recede. The A.B. Voorhis Hose Company No. 1, located at the corner of Walnut Street, towers over the street on the left. The fire bell hung above the third floor to call firefighters to duty. (KHS.)

Overcoats, gloves, fishing poles, lanterns, canned tomatoes, yams, apples, and onions are all on display at W.L. Thayer's general store, one of the many general stores providing supplies to residents of Canisteo. The proprietor (left) poses with a customer in front of the store. (KHS.)

The Great Atlantic & Pacific Tea Company, later known as the A&P, was on Depot Street. Here, puff wheat is 9¢ a package, river salmon is 14¢ a half pound or 23¢ a pound, creamy butter is 39¢ per pound, salad dressing is 20¢ a bottle, and crackers come in 4¢ and 8¢ packages. (KHS.)

The aprons of these men advertise a "manager special [on] Oleomargarine." This store was also located on Depot Street. Other things advertised here are washing powder, wheat croquet, chocolates, Lipton's tea, and Velvet, the smoothest tobacco. (KHS.)

The Gas Co. was located at 13 Depot Street, between the *Times* and the *Chronicle* newspaper businesses. Most businessmen at the time dressed in tailored suites with pocket watches and smoked cigars. The second floor was home to the Mutual Life Insurance Company. (KHS.)

A postal worker stands in front of a door with a mailbox to the left. Because of the reflection in the window, it is clear he is across Depot Street from the IGA. (KHS.)

These barbers pose with comb and scissors in hand in the doorway next to the barber post in 1916. The poster in the window advertises a track and field meet to be held at the Canisteo Academy on Election Day. (KHS.)

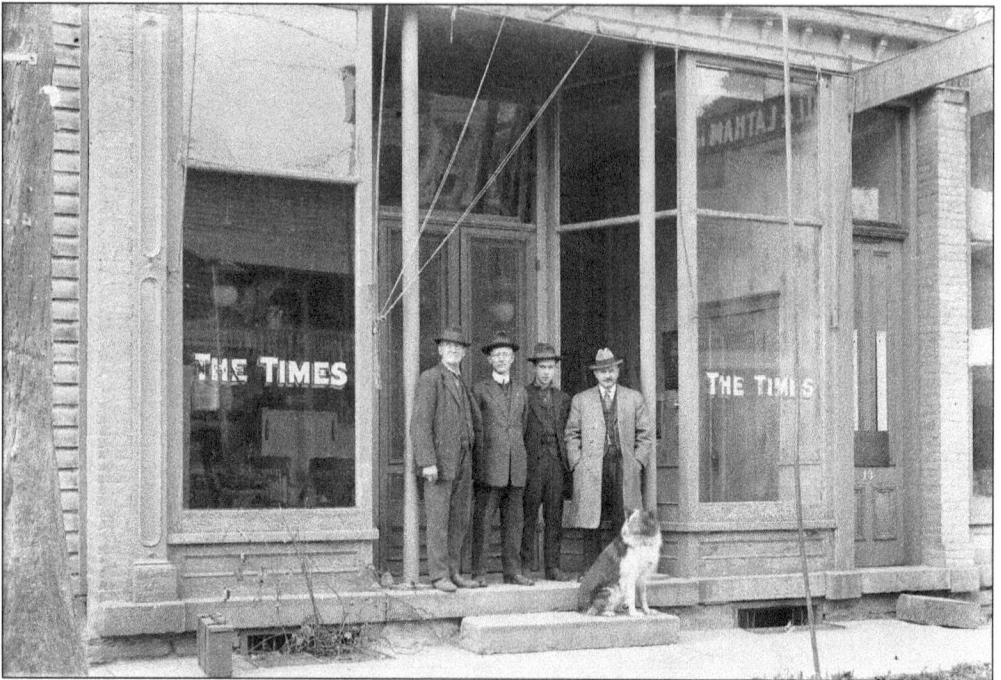

The *Times*, located on Depot Street, was founded in 1877 under the editorship of A.H. Bunnell and was the longest-running newspaper in Canisteo, printing its last paper in the early 1960s. Papers from 1880 on were hardbound and later microfilmed; they are now housed at the Kanestio Historical Society. The sign in the upper right corner reads Hall & Latham. (KHS.)

L.L. Hough's *Canisteo Chronicle*, also located on Depot Street, was in publication about the time of World War I. Only a few of the papers have surfaced, as the newspaper was only in circulation for a few years. The *Canisteo Republican*, another short-lived newspaper, was edited by E.G. Harris. (KHS.)

On the right, at the corner of Depot and Fourth Streets, is the Gillis Hotel. Today, the Canisteo Car Wash stands at this location. The hotel was a popular place to play pool and buy cigars. Attached to the left side of the building was one of Canisteo's bowling alleys. (KHS.)

The clock at the PK Cafe on Depot Street shows 2:20 p.m. in this photograph, taken shortly after electricity was installed. The cafe sign must have been a sight when it was first lit up. Candy jars sit on the counter just inside the front door, and a Beech-nut Tobacco advertisement is in the other window. The Kanisteo Laundromat, now closed, was later at this site. (KHS.)

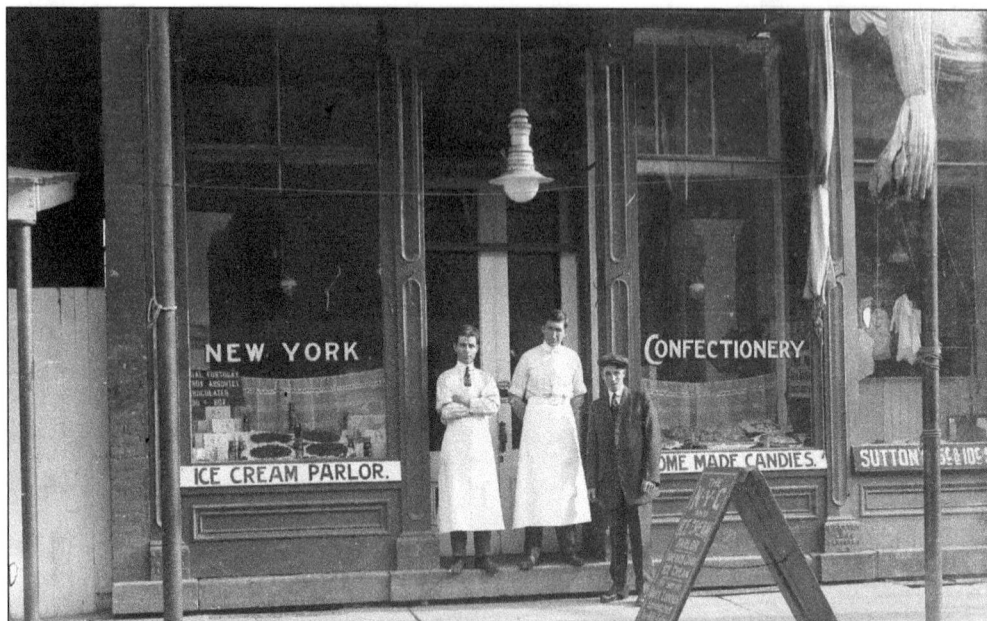

The New York Confectionery, an ice cream parlor and candy store, was located in the building that now houses the post office. Note the gaslights in both windows and the four columns on either side of the windows, which were cast at the Henry Carter & Son foundry farther down Depot Street. (KHS.)

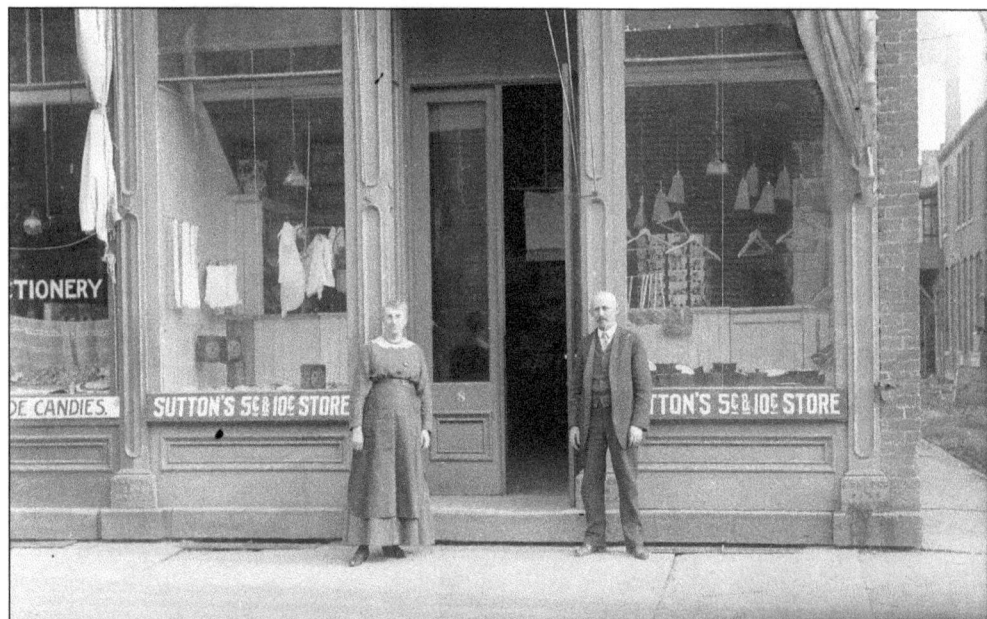

Next door, on the right side of the current post office, was Sutton's 5¢ and 10¢ Store. Judging by the jack-o'-lantern bags in the window, this photograph was likely taken around Halloween. Whisk brooms and coat hangers are on display in the window on the right. Coat hangers, a recent phenomenon in Canisteo, were popular items in stores around 1916 when this photograph was taken. (KHS.)

The Independent Order of Odd Fellows (IOOF) hall was on the third floor of this building, with the law office of Almon W. Burrell on the second and Mitchell's drugstore on the first. A jeweler occupied the portion near the large watch seen here, which is now home to a barbershop. Steuben Trust Company, the current owner of the building, occupies the front portion of the first floor. A trolley and trailer car awaits passengers for its next departure. (KHS.)

The Canisteo House, later known as the Manwell Block, was the first brick building in Steuben County. When the railroad came to Canisteo, Depot Street was built connecting the hotel with the new railroad depot, and it became the main business and manufacturing district. Note the band playing on the second-floor porch. (KHS.)

Now Citizen and Northern, the First State Bank opened for business on April 29, 1897, with cash on hand of $2,762.72, plus $460 in gold and $348 in standards. The first president was L.D. Whiting, who served until 1912. The granite columns and the lead-glass window are still familiar parts of the Main Street landscape. (KHS.)

A.J. Aronson's logo adorns the right door of his store. It is an arrow, followed by the letters "on" and a sun: Aronson. This was a popular clothing and shoe store in the early 1900s located on Main Street. Crawford Shoes, Fashion Park Cloths, Arrow Shirts, and Harvard Hats are a few of the brands that Aronson carried. (KHS.)

The men's department of the Rosenberg Store is seen here. The sign hanging from the ceiling reads, "Don't forget the boys." Elizabeth Bennett (left) worked in the women's department until that portion of the business was closed in the 1930s. Seen to the right of Bennett are, from left to right, salesman David Cohn, I.M. Rosenberg, and clerk Claude Wambold. (KHS.)

The women's department of the Rosenberg Store is seen here before World War I. Undergarments hang on the wall, and purses are in the center display case. The women's department sold patterns and carried bolts of material. Elizabeth Bennett is second from the left, and Rosanna Hipenstall is on the far left. (KHS.)

Seen here on Main Street is the M.N. Sammet & Bro. store. A clothing store carrying standard patterns, it has sample dresses in the left window. While the second window is vacant, men's ties and suits are in the next window, and shoes hang in the last window. (KHS.)

Wendell Wilkins, seen here in 1943, ran a well-known bicycle shop on South Main Street. In this photograph, the safe is open, and the cash register is ready for the next sale. The calendar behind him advertises another Canisteo business: Schnurle & Son Insurance, located at 5 West Main Street. (KHS.)

Zeltwanger's meat market is seen above when it was on the street level. The building, now a Chinese restaurant, was later raised up to protect it from flooding. Before the dikes were built following the flood of 1935, the village had many floods. At the time of this photograph, the stairs were in the ally on the left; they were later moved to the alley on the right. Beef was never precut or packaged, as can be seen below inside the meat market. Fish was kept in a wooden crate under the sides of beef. The calendar on the wall dates these photographs to 1912. (Both, GD.)

Many items are on display in front of the Goff hardware store, situated at the corner of West Main and Depot Streets, in 1916. The building was formerly the Allison Boot & Shoe Factory and the Stephens & Hitchcox Funeral and Furniture Store. To the right of the door is a grinding wheel and a bicycle. "Meeks Hardware" is written on the grinding wheel. (KHS.)

The man with the large mustache in this photograph is wearing an apron from Meeks Hardware. These men are possibly reviewing blue prints for the new Meeks building, which would be located at 19 Main Street. That building is currently vacant, but it was more recently occupied by a ceramic shop and a dollar store. However, it is best known as the hardware store. (KHS.)

The step entering the poultry supply store is made of two crates with a plank connecting them. It must be more solid then it appears, as the bags of seed in the right window each weigh 100 pounds. This building, located on South Main Street, was once a Laundromat and is currently the home of the Valley Salon. (KHS.)

Originally part of Flohr's tannery, the right side of this building served as service bays for the gas station next door. More recently, it has been a restaurant and bar for years, with many names over the years as it changed ownership. Some more memorable names included the Tannery, Baggie Knees, and the Filling Station; currently its name is Nick-L-Brew. (KHS.)

In the 1920s, Hoosier kitchen cabinets were quite popular, as seen here in the left window of Walter H. Brasted's furniture and undertaking business. Parlor furniture is in the other window, and wicker furniture is displayed in the second-floor window. Apparently, no one noticed the photographer, as the lady in the back of the car got caught wiping her nose. (KHS.)

This rear photograph, taken from the roof of the fire station, looks down the back alleys of the Main Street stores toward Depot Street. The three-story building with one awning on the second floor is the current post office building, which was owned by the Masons. When looked at closely, several outhouses are seen. (KHS.)

Floodwaters are seen here in 1889, rising up to the knees of the men on the left and right. The bandstand is on high ground, overlooking the park and the downtown square. The chimneys of the Stewart Hospital are in the background. The house to the right is Canisteo's town hall. The men are carrying brooms. (KHS.)

This building floats down Main Street in the 1889 flood. The far right of the image shows that part of the Canisteo Fire Department building completely collapsed. The men are attempting to rescue a piece of equipment. To the far left is a harness shop, and in the center is the Helms & Aber Boot & Shoe Shop. (KHS.)

EAST MAIN STREET, CANISTEO NY.

The first building on the right is the former Stewart Hospital, a private hospital at the corner of East Main and Elm Streets. Directly across the street, the first house on the left is known as the Mabel Cornish house. Note the porch that once adorned the front of her house. Communication wires hung over the right side of the street. (KHS.)

Dr. Harry J. Stewart (left) graduated from the University of Buffalo in 1901, and his son Dr. Harold O. Stewart (right) graduated from the same university 30 years later. The interior of Dr. Stewart's office, located at 6 East Main Street, was quite spacious. Note the certificate and the telephone on the wall. (KHS.)

The Stebbins photography studio is in the foreground in this view, looking down West Main Street (originally Hornellsville Street). The lower sign reads "Headquarters for Picture Framing," and the sign just down the street reads "Cleaning, Pressing, and Repairing." Farther down the street, two men dig a trench while a team of horses stands by. (KHS.)

Albert Benton "A.B." Stebbins won many state and national awards for photography, and was recognized by the Smithsonian Institute in Washington. Stebbins's studio was first located on Depot Street, but he later built his own studio on Main Street. The north wall of the second floor was made up entirely of windows, letting in natural light. Seen here is the back of one of his photographs, advertising his services. (KHS.)

The Wimodaughsian Library received its charter from the state in November 1897, with a membership of 24 women. First housed on the second floor of the current Steuben Trust building, it moved to the Manwell Block a decade later. It was then moved to the Grange building, situated at the corner of Maple and South Main Streets, before moving into this house, its current location, in 1933. (KHS.)

This photograph gives a glimpse into how children dressed in the early 1900s. Boys wore knickers, and it was common for girls to have a big bow in their hair. These children pose on the front lawn of Judge Joseph Latham's home, located at 23 West Main Street. The cobblestone porch was later enclosed. (KHS.)

This snowy scene shows Greenwood Street after a trolley passed through, along with several horse-drawn carriages. The Baptist church is on the left, and Canisteo's original schoolhouse was across the street from the church, followed by the Woodburn monument works, where William Sheeley's house now stands. (KHS.)

The current location of the miniature golf course on Greenwood Street was once home to Chancellor Cigars. In later years, it was the location of Cleveland's. At the time of this photograph, the Methodist steeple had been replaced with a decorative rail. Ice cream is still served at the corner store on the right. (KHS.)

The Walter Brasted furniture store was on Greenwood Street next to the Wesleyan church. Parlor furniture is seen here in the window, and a selection of baby carriages is on the sidewalk. The boy in front of the store wears roller skates and knickers, and the sides of Joe Brasted the Drayman's wagons advertise Hoosier kitchen cabinets. (KHS.)

Orton O. Lain's hardware store was well known and photographed often over the years. Located on Greenwood Street, this photograph shows potbelly stoves on display in the left window and gas heaters on the right. The sign on the right window reads Chi-Namel Store. Later occupied by Spencer Hardware and then Napa Auto Parts, the building has been vacant for many years. (KHS.)

From left to right, Henry Hollands, Pauline Stephens, and Ordway Stanton are seen here in Hollands Hardware, located at 20 Greenwood Street, in the 1940s. They sold a variety of hardware and household items. (KHS.)

"Another full truckload of GE appliances" is delivered by Cleveland's Truck Lines of Hornell, New York, to Hollands Hardware. The Hollands Hardware phone number, 2541, is seen on the side of the pickup truck on the right. (KHS.)

This 1991 photograph was taken not long before the Canisteo Movie Theater at the corner of Greenwood and Lain Street was torn down. The theater was open through the 1950s, with movies costing 10¢. The ticket booth is between the steps, under the projector room, which protruded from the front of the building. (KHS.)

This photograph looks north on Greenwood Street toward Depot Street. The Riddell Hall opera house was on the third floor above the Allison B. Laine Book Store. Alongside the bookstore were the coal office and the post office. The building with two chimneys is the Canisteo House hotel. Note the wooden sidewalks and the firewood piled in the street at the curve up the street. (KHS.)

The snow has been plowed from the streets and sidewalks as this couple walks to town. The house to the left is at the corner of Ninth and Greenwood Streets, and the one on the right is at the corner of Tenth and Greenwood Streets, across from the present elementary school. (KHS.)

Horses graze in the pasture just below the living Canisteo sign. The building of the elementary school in the 1950s changed the landscape below the sign. Today, the horse pasture is the school's cross-country course. The old alfalfa fields were leveled, making the hill behind the school much steeper. (KHS.)

The front lawn of Dr. George Preston's house was terraced facing Greenwood Street. The centralized school district used the first floor for homemaking classes and the second floor for administrative offices. For a period of time, the school's dental hygienist's office was on the second floor, above the bay window on the right. (KHS.)

This house, at 97 Greenwood Street, was once one of the most beautiful houses on the street. Before it burned in the late 1800s, it was the home of Lorada Vickers. At the time of this photograph, it appears to be in need of some repair, as the shutters are missing from one of the front parlor windows. Notice the widow's walk and the woman on the second-floor porch. (KHS.)

The New York & Pennsylvania (NY&P) tracks split into four directions as they crossed Third Street, seen here looking north toward the railroad yards. The Canisteo Cornet Band played several selections on November 1, 1896, when the NY&P ran its first excursion from Greenwood to Canisteo. Flood damage in 1935 ended the railroad. (KHS.)

The NY&P had a platform on East Academy Street to discharge and receive passengers going to and from the academy, just a couple blocks away. Students from as far away as the northern tier of Pennsylvania commuted by train to attend school at Canisteo. These passengers awaiting the train appear to be a bit older then school students. (KHS.)

A young boy on a bicycle poses with his parents outside their home at the end of Prospect Street, which is now owned by Mick and Jennifer Carretto. The porch was changed to make the front face Riddell Street, when Riddell was built to connect Prospect Street with West Academy Street. The house no longer sits on a corner lot. Note the crown at the roof's peak. (KHS.)

This band poses with their bouzouki guitars in front of the Hitchcox house, overlooking the village at the end of Fairview Place. The house was built in 1814 by Timothy Russell, the maternal grandfather of Mary S. (Stephens) Hitchcox, who lived there with her husband, Julius Hitchcox, a businessman and funeral director who operated a funeral business out of the castle on Russell Street. (KHS.)

During a flood on Green Street, two boys in the center of the street float around on boards used as rafts while another boy is neck-deep in the water in front of them. The streetlight is on the corner of Main Street, where the Hubertus Service Station stands today. Barns were once part of the landscape around town, but today are scarce. (KHS.)

In this photograph of a flooded Canisteo, the three houses in the middle are on Walnut Street. Note that the front doors of each are on the side. Behind the houses, lumber is stacked two stories high, likely for shipping. The Erie Railroad Bridge crossing the Canisteo River is in the distance, between the two barns. (KHS.)

Floods were a common occurrence in the village; this photograph looks down Taylor Street. Photographs like this one were regularly taken when flooding occurred, in order to document the damage. (KHS.)

The J.H. Strait Milling Company, located next to the New York & Pennsylvania Railroad crossing on Fifth Street, advertised flour, seeds, barley, hay, coal, wood, lath, lime, cement, brick, plaster, shingles, fertilizers, poultry food, and condition powders. Reitnauer Used Furniture occupied the site as late as 1989. (KHS.)

Men deliver milk to the Canisteo Creamery, built on Sixth Street in 1897. George Foldger was the manager from 1910 until it closed around 1930. Here, the man inside operates a lift to unload the milk cans from the wagon onto a set of scales in the building. Railroad tracks are alongside the building to the left. (KHS.)

A team of three mules with a heavy load of milk cans pauses at the Sixth Street New York & Pennsylvania Railroad crossing on its way to the Canisteo Creamery. The railroad crossing sign reads, "Look out for the cars." The canvas covering shades the milk cans from the hot summer sun. (KHS.)

Gordon Scott and his wife, Kathleen, owned Scott's Dairy, seen here. Schoolchildren often toured the plant to see how milk was pasteurized and bottled locally. As a treat, they were led into the cooler to taste the ice cream. Here, bottles are being filled at the far end of the bottling machine. Today, the Ryan family uses the facility for the packing and shipping of an online pest control product. (KHS.)

Scott's Dairy Bar now stands empty, a reminder of the sweet treats that used to await customers. Located at the corner of Walnut and Main Streets, it housed a full-service dairy bar with a drive-up window. Today, ice cream is enjoyed at the former Walter Flohr service station on East Main Street. (KHS.)

Mrs Van Schaick.

The exchange of calling calls between well-to-do ladies was a tradition carried over from France. Cards like the ones seen here were left behind following visits as a reminder of one's presence, and were popular in the late 1800s. They were printed in bright colors and written with hand-printed calligraphy; some were even adorned with ribbon and lace and a secret door. Today, the old calling cards have become collector's items. These cards belonged to two local ladies: Lana Van Schaick, who resided in the Four Square house at 2 Spring Street, and Minnie Scott, the aunt of Gordon Scott. (Both, SC.)

Minnie Scott.

THE ONLY ORIGINAL AND CELEBRATED

LATEST NEWS CIGAR

Warranted
Havana Filler
and Sumatra Wrapper.

Mild,
Rich and
Pleasant.

MANUFACTURED BY EDWARD L. ALLEN.
CANISTEO, N. Y.

Canisteo had a few cigar producers, including Edward L. Allen of Canisteo, which produced this advertisement. Tobacco was grown locally; however, the old tobacco barns have disappeared from the landscape. Havana and Sumatra tobacco were used to create the mild, rich, and pleasant smoke. (KHS.)

Canisteo Silk Co. Canisteo, N. Y.

This is an early postcard of the Canisteo Silk Co., originally known as the Huguet mill, on Russell Street. Jean Raffard came to the area from France with his family and was the first superintendent when the plant opened in 1904. The mill employed as many as 75 workers, mostly women spinning raw silk. (SC.)

Hatcheries were a big business in Canisteo. William Riddell operated the Black & White Poultry Co., seen here, on West Academy Street. The Hough hatchery was at the corner of Greenwood and Eighth Streets. Hatcheries were also located on Maple Street and on Tenth Street. There is also an old hatchery building on Jean Pearson's farm, south of the village on Route 36. (KHS.)

Wooden boxes with burlap tops were used to ship thousands of chicks each year from the Hough hatchery. In February 1906, a poultry show was held in the Woodbury building on Depot Street, attracting breeders from as far away as New York City. Dr. George Preston was mentioned in the *Canisteo Times* as a breeder of prize Hamburgs. (KHS.)

This photograph, looking down on the village from Burt Hill, shows the backsides of Depot and Main Streets. The Canisteo River and Ordway Lane are in the foreground, with barns that are long gone. The village has since stretched across the flats and is protected by the levee system built after the 1935 flood. The Methodist steeple is to the far left, while the steeple of the Presbyterian church and the smokestack from Flohr's tannery are nearby. The three-story building in the center is the Masons' building. The fields on the hillside behind the village are in the area of what is now Square Woods Drive. (KHS.)

Old photographs such as this one give a glimpse of the fashions around 1900. Here, the woman on the left wears a fur-collared overcoat and boots, and the lady on the right has a ruffled neckline and cuffs. Ladies' hats, popular at the time, were often adorned with flowers. (KHS.)

On the far left, an Erie Railroad boxcar is on the tracks just down the hill from this North Hornell Street residence. Many of the homes in this section of town were once hotels. The house displays two American flags, and a third one is on the front steps. (KHS.)

Flower arrangements can still be purchased at this location on Greenwood Street; B.K.'s Boutique replaced the IGA, seen here with canned goods stacked neatly on the shelves and the meat and poultry counter in the far back. Things have changed, as these were the days before bar codes, so the staff labeled each can. (KHS.)

The old Canisteo Memorial American Legion Post No. 846 has been replaced with a modern facility and banquet hall. An old military tank sits in the front lawn, surrounded by a ring of flag posts. The pavilion in the background still stands alongside the small brook that borders the property. (KHS.)

The original bridge that spanned Bennett's Creek was silver, and thus the bridge was named the Silver Bridge. The original green bridge, seen here, was replaced by a modern bridge, but it is still referred to as the Silver Bridge. Route 36 crosses it heading south out of the village. (KHS.)

Two

THE 1887 AND 1898 CANISTEO ARCHES FIREMEN'S PARADES

On September 14, 1887, Canisteo hosted a firemen's parade and invited guest companies from around Steuben County. The V.L. Parsons Commercial House, at other times known as the Park Hotel, was decorated for the day. In later years, the porches were removed, and the roofline was changed. Through the years, the building was also used by the grange and the library. Note the woman sitting on the railing of the second porch behind the waving American flag. (KHS.)

On August 8, 1887, these firefighters pose in the park in front of the bandstand. The firemen are dressed in their best and decorated with ribbons. Preparations began in July for the firemen's parade, which took place on September 14. In the background, some storefronts on Main Street have already started decorating for the event. (KHS.)

The *Canisteo Times* estimated that between 5,000 and 8,000 people came to the event. The sixth annual firemen's parade was a great success, Canisteo residence spent $450 to decorate the village for the event. John S. Williams of Buffalo came to Canisteo with a boxcar load of decorations. Some of the firefighters are seen here perched on the steps of the bandstand. (KHS.)

Visiting fire companies arriving on the train were first greeted by the Allison Boot & Shoe Factory's three-story arch, constructed out of shipping creates. Looking down Depot Street toward Main Street, two additional arches are visible at the end of the street. The cables supporting this arch are visible on the right. (CFD.)

Two years earlier, in 1885, the Canisteo Sash & Door Company formed. The company erected an arch out of doors on West Main Street, welcoming Wellsville's Genesee Hose Company. St. Joachim's steeple is seen in the background. The Taylor chair factory constructed its arch on East Main Street, although no photograph captured it. (CFD.)

Greenwood Street was adorned with this Waldo Hose No. 2 arch, welcoming Baldwin's Hose Company. The Methodist church is in the background. The Riddle Hall opera house was on the third floor of the building to the right. The girls in the foreground pose on the wooden crosswalks. (KHS.)

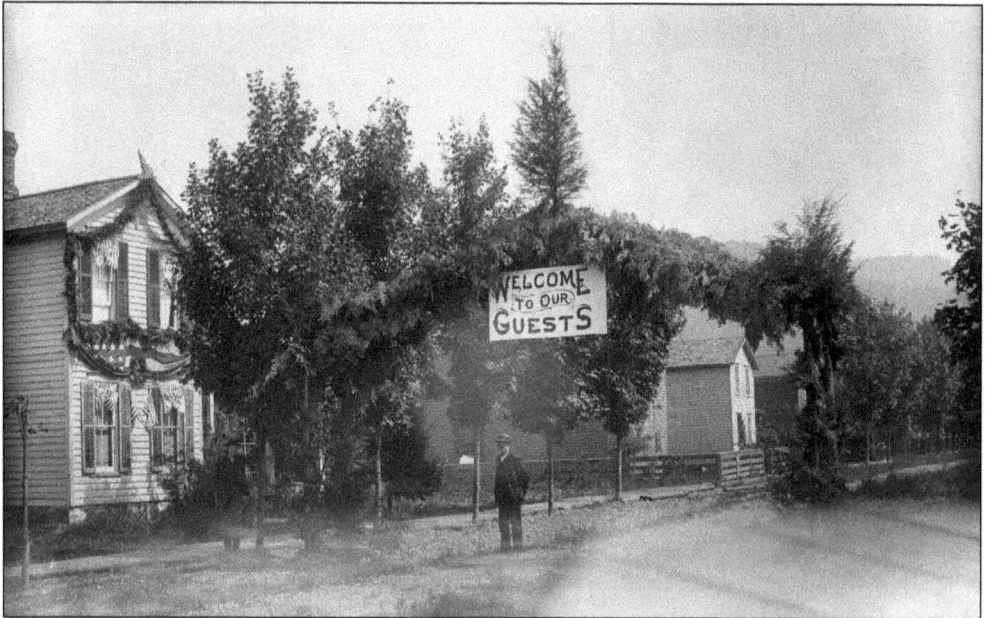

W.P. Delaney and G. Woodmansee constructed this arch on Taylor Street out of pine boughs. Mr. Breckenbridge, Mr. Beebe, and Albert Jeffers created an arch at the corner of Russell and Stephens Streets, and Mr. Neely, Mr. Basset, Mr. Goff, and Charley Dubois built one at the corner of Orchard and Stephens Streets. W.W. Goff's arch was on Russell Street. (KHS.)

The headquarters of F.N. Drake Hose No. 1 and Waldo Hose No. 2 is decorated for the event. Drake Hose used a couple of brooms on either side of their door as part of the decorations. The young boys on the left did not stand still long enough for the exposure. (KHS.)

The fire chiefs took up headquarters on the second floor of this Greenwood Street building, where Meyer's Floor Trendz is today. The second-floor bay window on the left would have been a great place to see the parade, which began and ended in front of this building. (KHS.)

The second and third floors of this building are still occupied by the Masons, while Canisteo's post office now occupies the first floor. A confectionery store and a five-and-dime once occupied the first floor. At one time, the right section of the third floor was used by the shoe factory. (KHS.)

Some of the finest equipment was on display in front of the Canisteo House hotel. Besides the arch on Greenwood Street, Waldo Hose No. 2 also welcomed Baldwin Hose Company here. A couple ladies pose on the second floor porch, while men brought out chairs to perch on the roof of the second-floor porch. (KHS.)

This photograph, looking west on Main Street, shows more arches set up to welcome other companies. The men of Canisteo's companies prepared several roman candles. Guests escorted to the depot in the evening said that the "heavens were fairly ablaze" during their time there. These arches were in front of the present historical society building on Main Street. (KHS.)

Even the Canisteo Academy got involved, as the children posed for this photograph. Their motto, hung up on the sides of the building, was "Our noble firemen, they protect our homes." Garland decorated the second and third floors, and double flags were hung over each of the first-floor windows. The parade passed by the academy twice, making it a good place to be as a spectator. (KHS.)

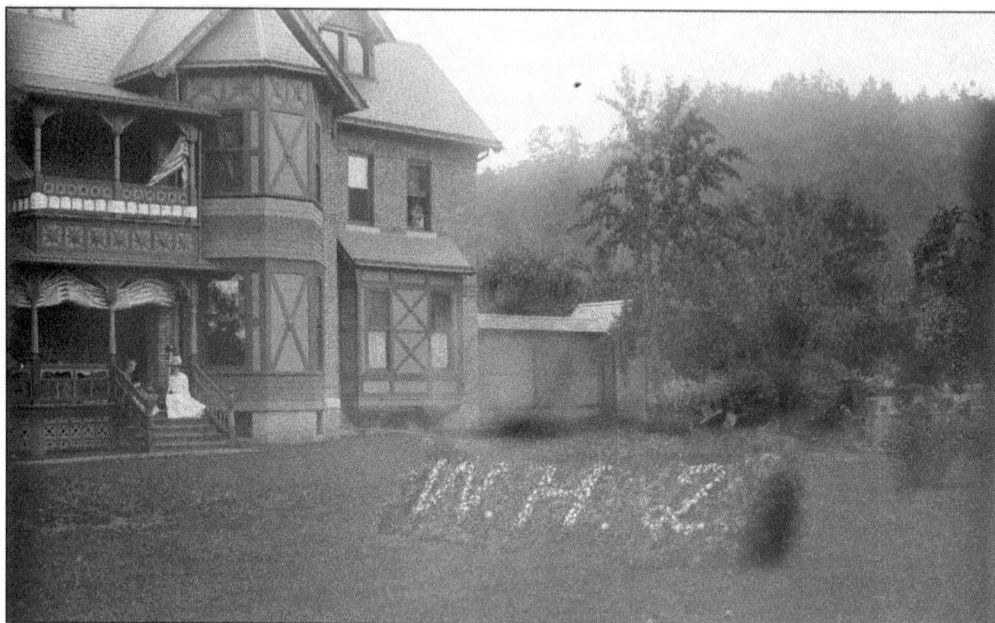

"W.H. 2" was planted in flowers to represent the Waldo Hose Company No. 2. Ladies sit on the steps of the house under the decorative banners. This brick house, located at 24 East Main Street, is now painted white. Pat and Patty Kelly now live in a house situated right where the "W.H. 2" was planted. (KHS.)

David Langley's house, situated at 18 East Main Street, is now a bed and breakfast operated by Sharon and John Cox. Paper lanterns adorn the front porch of the house in this photograph. A cast-iron fence is in the foreground, and an outhouse appears to be attached by an enclosed walk to the house in the background. (KHS.)

L.A. Waldo decorated his house at 12 East Main Street, positioned on the corner of Elm Street. The family poses on the front porch for this photograph. In later years, a second story was added to the right side of this house, and the roofline was changed. The brick house in the background has since been demolished. (KHS.)

Tom C. Doremus's house, located at 59 Depot Street, is currently an apartment house. The boy on the large tricycle is the only one not looking toward the photographer. Note the bandleader on the porch. (KHS.)

Each host fire company put together a feast for their guests following the firemen's parade and related events; the banquet hall of the Drake Hose Company was prepared for a banquet and decorated for the occasion. Commemorative ribbons were given to the companies and to fire police. The parade was led by marshal J.M. Hitchcox, and the Canisteo Steamer Company No. 1 brought up the tail. (KHS.)

Each company had prepared roman candles. While the companies were escorting their guests to the depot and firing off roman candles into the air, the Drake Hose arch took fire and had to be torn down. The arch had been strung with electric lights from the mill. The Allison Boot & Shoe arch is seen here in the background. (KHS.)

August 11, 1898, brought a new set of arches over the streets of Canisteo for another large firemen's parade, 11 years after the first. Headquarters occupied the second floor of the drugstore at the corner of Main and Depot Streets (now the Steuben Trust Company). The New York & Pennsylvania depot is in the far background. (KHS.)

Looking east down Main Street, this photograph shows horses in front of the fire station. The smokestack for Flohr's tannery reaches into the air in the background, just past the bell tower of the Drake and Waldo Fire Company building. The large building in the foreground with the American flags on the roof was once the Wilkinson store, but it is now a vacant lot. (KHS.)

71

Here, umbrellas are up to shade spectators from the summer heat. In the center is a piece of fire equipment. The trolley tracks are visible as well, as are the wires that support the heavy arches over the intersection. Other activities must be happening in the park, as the people in the foreground are facing that direction. An estimate of between 8,000 and 12,000 people attended the 1898 event. (KHS.)

This view, taken from Greenwood Street looking back toward Main Street, shows two of the arches. The horse is in front of what is now the Citizen and Northern Bank. The trolley tracks are visible at the crown of Greenwood Street, and a storm drain is in the foreground. (KHS.)

Many activities are seen in this photograph of the arches over Main and Greenwood Streets. A group of ladies (and one gentleman in the rear) is out for a bike ride while a couple of young girls look on. In the park behind the young girls is a woman with a baby stroller, and a group of men are engaged in conversation at the right. (KHS.)

In the late 1800s, bicycle clubs were popular. This group included, from left to right, Jesse McGeg, Maude Allen, Pearl Thacher, Nellie Harris, Nellie Betron, Pearl Walrath, Helen Riddell, and Bel Seeley. In the background, the trolley is seen with a trailer that was added to bring additional spectators from Hornell to Canisteo for the day's event. (KHS.)

The parade comes down Depot Street as the crowd falls in behind them. Awnings and umbrellas shade the storefronts and the people from the hot August sun. The Erie Railroad water tower is at the end of the street. To the right is the Stephens & Hitchcox furniture and general building supply business. (KHS.)

Depot Street businesses were also decorated for the occasion. This wagon is stopped in front of the J.B. Williams market. The Stebbins photography studio is seen here in its Depot Street location before it moved to Main Street. Schwarzenbach Beer of Hornell was a big advertiser at the event. (KHS.)

These images show the 1898 crowd gathered on the old baseball field next to the Depot Street river bridge to witness the judging of the drills. The men march in formation, seemingly in a circular motion. Most spectators sat on the ground, but some got a better view from the bridge. The drills were won by Addison, with Corning taking second place. The hose race was won by Honrellsville Erie, and Hornellsville Prindle took second. In the hub-to-hub race, Hornellsville Erie and Hornellsville Prindle tied for first place. The hook and ladder race was won by Perkinsville, with Corning Crystal taking second place. (Both, KHS.)

This photograph, looking west from in front of the Drake and Waldo Fire Company building, shows stores on Main Street. The piano and organ store is the current location of the Kanestio Historical Society. There is a tent at the end of the street, past the arch at Main and Greenwood Streets. Fireworks were enjoyed at the end of the event. (KHS.)

Three

GAS STATIONS AND GARAGES

The Garman Ford Agency, pictured here at 11 West Main Street, started in business around 1910. Later, in the 1920s, there were gas pumps on the curb, which can be seen on the right, selling Mobil gas. More recently, this building was the home of Rural Ministries before they moved to their present location in the former St. Ignatius Church. The building is currently a storage and shipping facility. (KHS.)

Located at the corner of West Main and Depot Streets, Al's Service Station was built in the 1930s. Ernest Davison operated it from 1938 to 1940, and it was later taken over by Albert Pfitzenmaier, who modernized it. His son Robert eventually became owner. Currently, it is the site of the Acorn gas and convenience store. (KHS.)

Gas can still be purchased from the Hubertus family at the corner of West Main and Green Streets. The original station at this location, operated by John Burns, opened in 1920 and sold Socony gas (now Mobil). (KHS.)

Ell's and Rod's Sunoco station, located at the corner of Main and Union Streets, was owned by Ells Henry and Rod Teribury. The present owner is Dave Harding. The first station was owned and operated by Otto Stephens, from 1933 to 1946, who sold Atlantic gas. Later, it was owned and operated for many years by Stephens's younger brother Kenny. This 1950s photograph shows a crew rebuilding the curbing in front of the station. (DH.)

The Taylor and Baker Garage was next to St. Ignatius Catholic Church. It was later home to Caple's Select Auto. John Burns's station is in the background. The mailbox in the foreground is at the corner of Walnut and Main Streets. (SC.)

Leon Burns started a Tydol station that was in business for many years at 47 West Main street, the present location of Canisteo Auto Mart. Burns also sold used cars. The station was torn down in the 1950s, and a new one was built, with living quarters for the owner/operator in part of the station. A.L. Schultz sold Rotary gas in the new station. (SC.)

The Esso station in the right background was operated by Kenneth Miller on West Main Street until it burned in the 1940s. The owner/operator lived above the service bays, which featured pits for mechanics to get under cars. An apartment building occupies that lot today. (SC.)

Jerry Peterson operated a gas station at 135 Greenwood Street in 1929. In 1930, Mr. and Mrs. Norton ran it until the couple's ill health caused them to close it. Their daughter Ruth Smith took over the property and sold Vitalized Keystone gas. The large house to the right was moved back from the street when the new Purdy Creek Bridge was built. (KHS.)

Gas pumps stood on both corners of Orchard and West Main Streets. The peeked part of Chauncey Watche's law office, seen here, was the original station, which opened in 1921 and was operated by Sergeant Miller until the 1940s. On the other corner was the Chevrolet agency and garage, which sold Esso gas and was originally operated by Jim Hendee. After him, Roland Harvey and Carl Gillis ran it, and Ken's Collision now occupies the property. (SC.)

Around 1930, on the northeast corner of Main Street and Ordway Lane, Seymour Mowers put up a gas station with a driving range behind it. In the early 1930s, it was bought by Raymond "Pat" Perkins, who sold Mobil gas there from 1933 to 1956. Seen here is the original building, which was moved to Fourth Street to make room for a newer structure and was later converted into a house. (SC.)

Robert M. Ellis Chevrolet Sales and Service proudly displays three automobiles for sale (from left to right): a 1924 Hudson, a 1927 Chevrolet, and a 1927 Pontiac. The NY&P Railroad tracks are seen at the left. This building was later home to a homebuilding business, which was replaced in the 1950s with the current structure, the site of an ATM manufacturing business. (KHS.)

The sign at Covell's Garage advertises automotive repairs and accessories. Covell's was located at 66 Depot Street. A hand tire pump is seen just inside the garage door. The man to the left enjoys his pipe, and the man in the center appears to be a businessman. The truck has a type of tank on its cargo bed, likely used to haul oil. (KHS.)

Four

SCHOOLS

The school at Willow Bend, district 11, is seen here on a brisk day. At the time, children likely only ever got their photographs taken for school pictures. These nine students surround their teacher in front of their school. (KHS.)

In this school photograph, eight boys and eight girls line up in order of height in front of their school, located at the foot of Gravel Run Road. The boys were required to remove their hats. The flag is missing from the flagpole, as are three shutters from the building. (KHS.)

It is hard to tell which person is the teacher in this photograph of the school at South Canisteo. Often, teachers were only a few years older than their pupils. This small schoolhouse must have been crowded, with 47 students in attendance on this day. South Canisteo was rural school district 10. (KHS.)

In the final years of the Swale school, pictured here, some changes occurred. The front awning was enclosed, and the back room was remodeled to include separate boys' and girls' toilet rooms, as mandated by the state. This is one of many rural schools that have vanished from the landscape. (GD.)

When schools centralized in 1937, many rural schoolhouses were neglected. The Bush Hill School was in need of repair in 1995. In some instances, rural schools became community buildings for the outlying areas. Originally, this school had a woodshed to its right side. (KHS.)

School district 2 was located in Hallettsville, between Stephens Gulf and Bakers Gulch Roads on Route 119. The school sat in front of the barn on the Sills property. This photograph was taken in the late 1970s, before the school was razed. The property is currently part of the Sills farm. (TO.)

The flag is hung beside the front door as 14 Adrian children posed on the front steps of their school in the late 1920s. The Adrian school had two classrooms, separated by a two-sided bookcase that housed the community's library. It also had a large foyer and attached outhouse bathrooms. (JC.)

The Oak Hill school, situated in the northeastern corner of Canisteo Township, was converted into a hunting cabin long ago. It is located near the three-point intersection where Oak Hill Road meets Nicholson and Cotton Roads. Because it is so close to Howard and Bath Townships, many people forget this region is part of Canisteo Township. Oak Hill was school district 7. (KHS.)

The many windows brightened the old Carter school, located on Route 248 towards Greenwood. Here, around 2000, the shutters in the bell house are deteriorating, along with some of the clapboards. At one time, electricity was run to the building, as evidenced by the attachments to the front. (KHS.)

The old elementary school, seen here, was on Fifth Street, where the Canisteo Manor stands today. This school was in use until a new one was built on Greenwood Street in 1914. Quite a few of these children appear to be barefooted, and a few teachers look out of the second-floor windows. (KHS.)

The old elementary school is seen here on the left from the top of the fire station in this view looking down the old millrace. The New York & Pennsylvania Railroad eventually ran through town alongside the millrace. The boys appear to be playing baseball on the left side of the school, while girls play under a shade tree in front of it. (KHS.)

This teacher had a full classroom with 33 students. The girls are all gathered in the front, with the boys in the back. Inkwells can be seen on the desks, and there is a map of Canisteo drawn on the chalkboard. (KHS.)

The Canisteo Academy (center) was erected in 1871, and the grade school (left) was built in 1914. The academy building was razed to make way for the present school building, erected in 1937, which is attached to the old grade school structure. The structure to the right, which later became known as the Preston House, accommodated the school's administrative offices and homemaking classes. (KHS.)

Canisteo's 1931 football team included, from left to right, (first row) Chilton Latham, Loyal Vandyke, Alfred Slawson, Karl Zeltwanger, Richard Kline, Arthur Wells, Robert (second row) I.N. Rosenberg, Orville Van Zile, Bill Carrier, Darwood Burns, John Boller, Lloyd "Red" Smith, and coach Lloyd "Gus" Larson. Football is still played in the fall at the central high school. This photograph shows the old style of uniforms and helmets. (KHS.)

The new grade school on Greenwood Street was erected in 1914. This facility still stands as part of the current high school, which was added onto the building in 1937. The boys are on the left side, and the girls are on the right. In the second- and third-floor windows are quite a few plants, perhaps the result of a science project. (KHS.)

These grade school children play a game in the school lawn. The girls are on the perimeter circling the boys, while the girl to the left is getting ready to throw a football at the boys. This photograph offers a great view of the fire escape at the Canisteo Academy. (KHS.)

Canisteo schools centralized in 1937 after the completion of this building, which originally housed all grades. Since that time, a few additions have been constructed, extending the back of the building by adding more classrooms, including a first-floor expansion into the center courtyard. Today, it houses grades eight through twelve. (KHS.)

In 1959, the new elementary school was built under the living Canisteo sign. This facility housed kindergarten through fourth grade and provided much-needed relief to the overcrowded main building. The new facility included a pool, opening the opportunity for swim classes. A two-story addition has been added since this photograph was taken, along with a modern gym. Currently, students from prekindergarten through seventh grade are schooled at the facility. (KHS.)

Five

CEMETERIES

Headstones fade after many decades in the open elements of weather. This headstone, in Baker Cemetery, belongs to Revolutionary war hero Jeremiah Baker, who died in 1825 at age 78. His wife, Anna, died a year later. She was also 78. When the couple was younger, Anna was captured by Indians in the Wyoming Massacre. Fortunately, her husband rescued her. (SC.)

This stone tells the story of the 1825 death of Joshua Stephens, who was 32 years old: "In the seal of retirement in friendship and love; many choice blessings are sent from above; on that bold morning his prospects were bright; his wife and his children was all his delight; ere the sun had returned in the western main; by a ball from a rifle unarmed he was slain." (SC.)

The Bennett's Creek stone below references this man's occupation but does not list his birth or death year. "In memory of Thial Clark the jeweler who has quit running. But is wound up in hopes of being taken in hand by the supreme grandmaster mechanic for repairs and to be readjusted and set running in the world to be. So mole it be. Aged 75 years." (SC.)

Following World War I, there was a flood of immigrants to this country from Europe. In the 1920s, the Ku Klux Klan was at its peak of membership. A couple of stones can be found in Woodlawn Cemetery indicating membership in the local chapter, which consisted of businessmen and clergymen against minority groups coming from Europe. (SC.)

The Marsh monument greets guests as they enter Hillside Cemetery. There are three cemeteries in the village of Canisteo: Woodlawn, Hillside, and Pioneer. All three border each other and appear to be one large cemetery. Pioneer, the oldest, is no longer active, while Hillside and Woodlawn were both established in the 1880s. This life-size monument stands five feet and five inches tall. (SC.)

The Lorenzo Davison headstone, located in the center of Hillside Cemetery, is the largest monument in the town, with a 7-foot base and towering 20 feet into the trees. The town of Canisteo has 13 cemeteries, along with a few family-owned burial grounds. The Adrian Cemetery was abandoned, and all the stones were removed, while a few Indian burial grounds have been unearthed over the years and left unmarked. (SC.)

Six

CHURCHES

The First Presbyterian Church stands proud at the corner of South Main and Maple Streets, overlooking the park. It was established in 1836, and Canisteo's first church building was built in 1853. The steeple and bell were added later in 1856. The manse is seen here on the right, with a beautiful wraparound porch. (KHS.)

The first service in the Wesleyan church was held on May 18, 1935, in the partially completed building on Greenwood Street. A three-story building at the corner of Main and Depot Streets was purchased and torn down to provide materials, including the oak finishing for the sanctuary. The parsonage is behind the church, at 6 Maple Street. (SC.)

The steeple spirals into the air over the Methodist church, built in 1856. The steeple above the two-step bell tower got struck by lightning and had to be removed. It was replaced with a decorative rail, which was removed long ago as well. The lot where the brick house sat is now the church parking lot. Canisteo Christian Nursery School is held in the addition at the back of the church. (SC.)

The altar of the First Baptist Church is decorated for children's day. This photograph was taken before the pipe organ was installed. The property was purchased in February 1878, and the church was dedicated in December 1880, almost three years later. The original parsonage, on Russell Street, was sold, and the second parsonage was the house to the east of the church. Today, the parsonage is the brick house to the west. (KHS.)

St. Joachim's Church was dedicated on November 20, 1880, with bishop Stephen Vincent Ryan, the second bishop of Buffalo, giving the sermon. There were only about 15 Catholic families in Canisteo before 1880. The numbers grew following the opening of the church, as evidenced here in this 1916 confirmation class. (KHS.)

At the time this photograph was taken, this was the residence of Lorenzo Davison, a prominent businessman who died in 1900. After his death, the entire front page of the *Canisteo Times* was dedicated to his accomplishments. Today, his residence is best known as the Galeazzo Civic Building, and its current owner is the Faith Independence Baptist Church, located at 10 Maple Street. (KHS.)

The Kingdom Hall of Jehovah Witness building has expanded in recent years to accommodate the growing congregation. Located on Dunning Road just outside of the village limits, the Christian denomination is known for its translation of the Bible, called the *New World Translation of the Holy Scriptures*. (SC.)

Prior to the building of Spring Brook Church, South Canisteo residents held church services at the school. Once Spring Brook was built, they were no longer permitted to meet in the school. The cornerstone reads "Methodist Protestant Church 1894," reflecting when work began on the South Canisteo church. Four reverends were on hand to assist the resident pastor with the dedication ceremony. (KHS.)

Swale's Union Church, erected in 1893, was in a sad shape of disrepair and had to be dismantled in the late 1960s. It was located on Route 30, next to the Swale Cemetery. Here, Chicago corporate attorney Delbert White (left), home for a visit, pauses with Monroe Dickey on the west stoop of the church on a late summer afternoon. (GD.)

The First Free Will Baptist Church was erected in Adrian and dedicated on Christmas Day 1868. The original deed shows that the Methodist Episcopal Church had free use of the church edifice. Seen here in the 1950s is the Sunday school, under the leadership of superintendent Victor Howland. With a two-step bell tower, the steeple was never added. (SC.)

The building below was originally intended as a house but was never finished. Some residents in the Adrian vicinity purchased it in the early 1980s and, after renovations, opened up the Canisteo Valley Church of Christian Fellowship. The church is of Protestant affiliation and is an active part of the Adrian community. (SC.)

Seven

THE TOWN

Perched high upon the hill along the back road between Canisteo and Hornell, the photographer looks down on Dr. Spencer Annabel's farm. The photograph is a stereograph card, one of several taken around the Canisteo area. The children sit on the fence, and there are picnic tables under the shade trees. The barn to the right no longer stands, but the other buildings are still part of the farm. (KHS.)

The house on the far left is currently at the corner of the McGee and McBurney Roads in Bell Haven. The Canisteo town line cuts across the flats to the right edge of the cherry tree orchard in the foreground. The next farm to the right, with the barn with white doors, is now the home of James and Ruth Whitmore. The next farm to the right belongs to the Dineen family. (KHS.)

Calbraith Perry Rodgers made the first coast-to-coast flight, starting out from Sheepshead Bay, New York, on September 17, 1911. He landed in the Dineen fields just outside of Canisteo on September 22. The flight took him to Los Angeles, California, a 3,220-mile trip, and he landed on November 5. The airplane was named the *Vin Fiz* for the new soft drink the Armour Meat Company was promoting. (KHS.)

Obes Glen, named after Obadiah Stephens, was found to be a good source of slate for sidewalks, stair treads, and tombstones. The quarry, seen here in the 1930s, does not look like much, but some of the old slate sidewalks are still visible around the village. A couple of the tombstones are still visible in the woods near the site of the old quarry. (KHS.)

A horse and carriage passes over the old bridge that carried Route 119 over the tracks beginning in the 1850s. The bridge was replaced in the 1990s with a modern one that gives the trains more clearance. Today, only a single track passes under the bridge as it makes its way through the valley. (KHS.)

In the early 1900s, the Arts and Crafts style of home became popular. Many homes were purchased by mail order catalog and arrived in boxcars on the Erie Railroad. This house was purchased from the International Mill and Timber Company of Bay City, Michigan, and called the Superior. Its current owners are Brent and Beth Rauber, and it was originally built on the site of the Stephens' burned former house. (SC.)

Seen here in 1952 is the bridge that leads across Bakers Gulch Creek to the Canisteo Rod and Gun Club. The club, incorporated in 1907, leased the present location from the late 1920s until it purchased the land in 1949. The clubhouse was erected in 1936. These two sisters are Patricia Eldridge and Joanne Koon. (SC.)

Once known as the Methodist Park, the Baker Memorial Cabin was built in 1924 along Baker's Gulch. The cabin has since been converted into a private residence by the Jamison family. Behind the cabin was a tabernacle that tragically came down one night when a horse tied to it spooked, breaking loose one of the corner poles. (KHS.)

The first settlers in the Canisteo area took lots drawn by straw. Richard Crosby drew the straw for lot 12, situated in the eastern part of the original township. Upon his death in 1824, lot 12 was divided into what first became known as Crosby Thirds and later Crosbyville. Today, it is known as Adrian. Note the address on this 1850s envelope. (SC.)

Enoch Ordway, the owner of the Adrian House hotel in Crosbyville, donated land to build the depot above in an agreement with the railroad that he would name it, which he did, after his hotel. Thus, mail being delivered via train was addressed to Adrian, and the name of the hamlet changed. In the background are the railroad's shipping barn and signal tower, and a caboose departs down the tracks. (SC.)

Clara Jackson hangs Adrian's mail from this wooden arm. Her husband was the station agent and she was the postmistress and the general store proprietor. Neither could leave their post when the mail train passed through, so they trained their bird dog Sport to retrieve the mailbag and take it to the store for timely mail delivery. The wooden mail arm was later replaced by a steel arm. (KHS.)

This 1938 photograph shows a typical rural winter scene around Canisteo, with a New York Telephone Company repair truck headed out to service the lines following a big storm. The snow is piled almost as high as the truck. The advertisement on the back of the truck reads, "Telephone Appointments, Prevent Disappointments; Telephone Ahead." The bottom of the license plate advertises the 1939 New York World's Fair. (KHS.)

In this 1917 photograph, a young man waves goodbye from the rear of a departing caboose that is taking him and many other young men off to serve their country. Trains were the main form of public transportation, carrying many local young men off to war. (KHS.)

Use LAUTZ BROS & CO's
Best Bar Soap made
ACME SOAP
(Cut Full Pounds.)

This 1880s business card for J.W. March, a dealer in dry goods, groceries, notions, and tobacco, advertises Acme Soap. Passing out these cards was a popular way to get a name out to customers. These cards were hand-colored to bring out the details. J.W. Marsh's store was lost to fire in July 1886. The fire started in a storage shed attached to the back of the store. There was a fear of losing the house across the street because of high winds, but the bucket brigade kept pouring water on the house, saving it from the fire. (Both, SC.)

J. W. MARSH,

-----:) DEALER IN (:-----

Dry Goods, Groceries, Notions. Tobacco, &c., &c.

ADRIAN, N. Y.

Use LAUTZ BROS. & CO'S ACME SOAP !

Best Bar Soap Made.   Cut full Pounds.

This 1892 artist's sketch shows the Railroad House hotel and sample room, located at the corner of Depot Street and Railroad Avenue. The sample room was the hotel's bar and barbershop, operated by the Eveland family. The old barroom had originally been a general store. The building was directly across the tracks from the Adrian depot. (SC.)

Harvey Ploof is seen here in 1940 with five rattlesnakes—two yellow and three black. Ploof lived on Wood Spur Road in Adrian, next to the railroad tracks, and was best known for his skill in catching rattlesnakes. It was said that he would take them to the bar for free drinks. Now on the extinction list, timber rattlesnakes are found only in the northeastern corner of Canisteo and are illegal to kill. (CC.)

In 1916, oil was discovered in Adrian, just across the river over the Catatunk Bridge on the Stanton farm. Oilmen came to the small hamlet from as far away as Pittsburgh and Philadelphia. The oil was amber in color and said to be so pure that locals ran it in early farm equipment without refining it. The oil flowed without needing to be pumped, and two additional holding tanks had to be brought in to catch the oil. A second well was put down on the flats behind the depot with no success. (Both, KHS.)

In the late 1860s, Brown's Crossing was known as Allen's Station. The Maple Lodge, seen here, was a popular hunting lodge run by Matthew S. Dickey. A ladder is propped up in the apple tree to the left, Hannah (Reese) Dickey holds her favorite cat, and the springhouse and other outbuildings are on the right. (GD.)

People play croquet on the front lawn (far right) of the Spring Brook farm. The beautiful Victorian house no longer stands, but the lawn is peppered with mature maple trees. To the left of the house are fruit trees, and the maple trees are still less then two stories high in this photograph. (KHS.)

To harvest honey, hives would be smoked, necessitating the wood supply seen at the base of the hill of this beehive farm, located on Rock Run Road near South Canisteo. The lady is likely holding a jar of honey, and written on one of the crates next to the shed (bottom left) is "Ross Jamison." (KHS.)

Bowlesville was located on Route 36, on the way to South Canisteo. In the distance is the first steam sawmill in the valley, owned by Thomas Bowles. The Holstein Association stock show and sales building now stands on the site of the old sawmill. Across the road were several small dwellings for the sawmill employees. The house in the foreground belonged to Edward R. Gay. (KHS.)

Improvements to the state highway changed South Canisteo's appearance. The building in the background to the left was the schoolhouse, known as the Rowling school. The barn in the foreground advertised Peck's Hardware in Hornellsville. A blacksmith shop, mercantile, and creamery were some of the businesses in the hamlet. (KHS.)

When finances were good, George Winn built this larger barn to house his blacksmith business. The original sign, which hung at the top of the shop, has weathered. This barn was used as a billboard, with advertisements painted on the sidewalls and roof. The sign on the front advertises J.M. Carter's groceries and meats. (TO.)

Below, the Winn family poses in front of their house in South Canisteo. The railing is missing from the second-floor porch, and there is a washbasin at the corner of the porch to catch rainwater for laundry day. The street runs close to the house, leaving a narrow front lawn. (TO.)

Horse-drawn sleighs were used on the snow-covered streets in front of the Wilson and Talbot Store in South Canisteo in January 1908. These men are dressed warmly, and the horses are covered with blankets to fight off the cold temperatures. The general store was a great place to pick up supplies and to socialize with neighbors. (GD.)

Canisteo's current town historian, George Dickey, is seen here on the Swale with his grandfather Louis Burns, boiling down maple sap into syrup. Dickey would come home from school and gather sap in milk cans, and the weekends were spent processing it. One of the old sap buckets is hanging from the tree at the left. (GD.)

Cool weather and a fresh snow meant it was hog-butchering time on the Swale. With two hanging in the shed and two outside, it was hard work and involved both the women and men. The jacket of the man to the left seems in need of mending as he holds the saw in preparation for processing the hogs. (GD.)

A good old-fashioned barn raising takes place on the Swale. A man stands at each upright post, waiting for the next beam to be guided into place. The visitor in the buggy obviously did not realize the photographer was taking a picture, as his back is to the camera. The women stopped for the photograph, as everyone got involved in the day's event. (GD.)

In this March 1906 image, Bennett's Creek Road is rutted from the winter thaw. In the background, debris from the creek has washed into the fields. This boy hauls a load of manure. Once he got to the field, he would rack his load out the back, and the manure would fall between the slats and onto the field. (GD.)

This photograph shows the building of Route 248, just below Bennett's Creek Cemetery near the Canisteo-Greenwood town line. The New York & Pennsylvania tracks were a single-line track through the Bennett's Creek valley. A second set of rails is on the right. (KHS.)

Many deeds in the 1800s actually dictated that the property be fenced with good board and post. The outhouse, a necessity of rural life, is on the far left behind the house. It was also typical of the day for women to wear hats to shade them from the hot sun. This house, located at 4038 State Route 248, is pictured before the road was raised when the new bridge was constructed. (KHS.)

Hops were a common crop to flavor beer, and they are seen here growing on this building. These two women shade the baby from the hot afternoon sun. Infant fruit trees adorn the front lawn, and the grass is not mowed. Lawnmowers were not mass-produced until 1870 and did not fully catch on until around 1900, so this was a typical country lawn of the time. (KHS.)

This image overlooks the valley and shows the hills in the background stripped of their lumber. The steam engine on the right chops corn and sends it into the silo by a grain elevator. Besides horses, teams of oxen were also used, as seen to the right. Local farmers came together at harvest time; here, right in front of the steamer, a man holds a small child to view the operation. (KHS.)

SULPHUR SPRINGS, CANISTEO, N.Y.

Waterfalls are common in the many creeks that feed into the Canisteo River. The most-photographed falls are Obes Glen Falls, north of Carson, and the falls at Fall Creek, on Route 248. This postcard shows the waterfalls known as Sulphur Springs. The creeks and waterfalls are still a nice place to cool off on hot summer days. (KHS.)

Purdy Creek Road is seen here just after it was rerouted, when the Route 248 bridge was replaced in the early 1960s. The original road ran between the creek and the houses. The last house on Greenwood Street on the right and the first house just past the road were both moved to their present locations during the construction of the new bridge. (SC.)

This barn was located just outside the village limits at the foot of Square Woods Drive. Changes in agriculture over the years have put small farmers out of business. As a result, barns such as this one have disappeared from the landscape. In fact, this one was burned by the fire department for practice in the late 1960s. (CFD.)

Workers put the finishing touches on the exterior of the Kanestio Historical Society building in 1995. The bricks were reclaimed street bricks from the sidewalk in front of the building. The corner posts are Carter & Son foundry posts, reclaimed from the row of Depot Street stores. An old grist wheel is part of the entrance floor. (KHS.)

ABOUT THE KANESTIO HISTORICAL SOCIETY

The Kanestio Historical Society was organized on August 20, 1984, by Betty Dennis, Marjorie Van Hyning, and Virginia Dickey. An interim board of directors was appointed until the first elections could be held. Regular meetings were held in the civic rooms of the Galeazzo Building, located on Maple Street, on the third Tuesday of each month. Collection material was housed in the second floor of the town hall. Later, the society took up temporary housing at 29 Main Street. At that time, they purchased the vacant lot at 23 Main Street. The community came together to build a modern two-story facility with the words "Kanestio Historical Society" written in the brickwork across the front of the building. The front facade was constructed from reclaimed material from around the region.

The society is chartered under the New York State Department of Education and received its provisional charter in June 1995 and an absolute charter in July 2001. To give the community a better understanding of the democratic way of life, it is important to understand that local history is the groundwork for understanding state and national history. This society exists to bring together people interested in Canisteo's unique history. Since moving into the facility at 23 Main Street in the fall of 1995, it has housed a museum reflecting life in the bygone days.

The purpose of the society is to preserve and display artifacts, relics, documents, photographs, books, and other historical items related to the history and culture of the Canisteo Valley. It also develops and conducts educational programs that convey the history and culture to both schoolchildren and the general public.

The society is open to the public Wednesday through Friday from 1:00 p.m. until 3:00 p.m., and other times by appointments. Educational programs and meetings are held on the third Tuesday of each month at 7:00 p.m., and the public is always welcomed. The facility is also available upon written request and approval from the board as a meeting place for other Canisteo-based organizations.

Inquiries can be made at P.O. Box 35 or by calling (607) 698-2086.

Visit us at
arcadiapublishing.com

www.ingramcontent.com/pod-product-compliance
Lightning Source LLC
Chambersburg PA
CBHW080606110426
42813CB00006B/1422